GAO

U.S. GOVERNMENT ACCOUNTABILITY OFFICE

441 G St. N.W.
Washington, DC 20548

March 4, 2014

The Honorable Carl Levin
Chairman
The Honorable John McCain
Ranking Member
Permanent Subcommittee on Investigations
Committee on Homeland Security and Governmental Affairs
United States Senate

The Air Force's Evolved Expendable Launch Vehicle Competitive Procurement

This report formally transmits the briefing slides we provided on January 28, 2014, in response to your request to examine issues related to the Department of Defense's (DOD) efforts to introduce competition into Evolved Expendable Launch Vehicle (EELV) acquisitions. The EELV program is the primary provider of launch vehicles and services for U.S. military and intelligence satellites. EELVs are also used to launch civilian and commercial satellites. The most recent independent cost estimate projects the program will cost about $70 billion through 2030.[1] From 2006 to 2013, the program acquired launch services from a single provider—the United Launch Alliance (ULA)—using a two-contract structure, but had little insight into EELV launch costs. In December 2013, DOD signed a contract modification with ULA, committing the government to buy 35 launch vehicle booster cores over a five-year period, and the associated capability to launch them.[2] The contract modification also covers all activities previously funded by the two-contract structure, and represents significant effort on the part of DOD to negotiate better launch prices through its improved knowledge of contractor costs. In addition to the 35 cores DOD is committed to buy from ULA between fiscal years 2013 and 2017, DOD has set aside up to 14 launches for competition among all certified launch vehicle providers.[3] DOD is currently developing a methodology for comparing launch proposals for the competition, which is expected to begin in fiscal year 2015.

This report addresses the following: (1) What insight did DOD have into launch costs under past EELV contracts? (2) How do recent changes to EELV contracts affect accounting for costs? (3) How is DOD compensated for costs when ULA sells launches to other customers? and (4) What are the implications if DOD requires competitors to submit offers using the same structure it currently uses with ULA or a commercial approach?

---

[1] The Office of the Secretary of Defense, Cost Assessment and Program Evaluation conducted an independent cost estimate based on the EELV programmatic forecast dated June 2012.

[2] The booster core is the main body of a launch vehicle. In the EELV program, common booster cores are used to build all of the Atlas V and Delta IV launch vehicles. Medium and intermediate launch vehicles use one core each, while the Delta IV Heavy launch vehicle requires three.

[3] Launch providers can become certified by following the steps outlined in the 2011 Air Force Launch Services New Entrant Certification Guide.

To determine the insight DOD had into launch costs under past EELV contracts, we reviewed the two most recent EELV Launch Services (ELS) and EELV Launch Capability (ELC) contracts and examined the contract structure and breakdown of costs included in the contracts. We received an in-depth verbal and written briefing on the ELC contract from DOD, and discussed with senior officials the history, context, and makeup of the EELV contracts. We interviewed DOD and ULA contractor officials regarding direct launch vehicle and other supporting activities performed under the contracts, and reviewed Defense Contract Audit Agency audit reports of EELV launch contracts, with report dates ranging from 2005 to 2012. We also reviewed past GAO reports and identified previous recommendations and their implementation to determine DOD insight into contracts. To determine how recent changes to EELV contracts affect accounting for costs, we reviewed sections of the new EELV contract with DOD and ULA contracting officials, received an in-depth DOD briefing on the structure of the new contract, and compared the contents and dollar values of the previous and current EELV contracts. To determine how DOD is reimbursed for costs when the incumbent provider sells launches to other customers, we examined ELC contracts from fiscal years 2012-2014 to identify reimbursements, we interviewed DOD and ULA officials to identify how amounts were calculated and the extent to which ELC costs were included, and we analyzed the reimbursement amounts and calculated the percentages of total ELC costs that the reimbursements represented annually from fiscal years 2009-2013. To determine the implications of possible DOD approaches to comparing launch proposals between the ULA and new launch providers, we reviewed draft DOD performance work statements related to the proposed EELV competition, and discussed the implications of DOD's plan with DOD officials, ULA and new entrant launch service providers. We also reviewed the Federal Acquisition Regulation (FAR) requirements for various types of contracts, including fixed-price and cost-type contracts. We conducted this performance audit from July 2013 through March 2014 in accordance with generally accepted government auditing standards. Those standards require that we plan and perform the audit to obtain sufficient, appropriate evidence to provide a reasonable basis for our findings and conclusions based on our audit objectives. We believe that the evidence obtained provides a reasonable basis for our findings and conclusions based on our audit objectives.

In summary, while the previous two-contract structure met DOD's needs for unprecedented mission success and an at-the-ready launch capability, the scope of its cost-reimbursement contract limited DOD's ability to identify the cost of an individual launch, as, according to DOD, direct launch costs were not separated from other costs.[4] For example, DOD paid for hardware through a firm-fixed-price contract (ELS), but funded infrastructure and engineering support through a cost-plus-incentive-fee contract (ELC).[5] The ELC cost-reimbursement contract was not transparent according to DOD officials, who had limited understanding of the activities funded under this contract. Additionally, minimal insight into contractor cost or pricing data meant DOD may have lacked sufficient knowledge to negotiate fair and reasonable launch prices. Coupled with uncertainties and possible instability in the launch vehicle industrial base, EELV program costs were predicted to rise at an unsustainable rate.

---

[4] In July 2011, the EELV program awarded a Launch Capability contract as a cost-plus incentive fee contract; the prior Launch Capability contract was a cost-plus award fee contract. A cost-plus incentive fee contract is a type of cost reimbursement contact that pays the contractor for allowable costs to the extent prescribed in the contract, and allows for the initially negotiated fee to be adjusted later, based on a formula in the contract. The fee is based on the relationship of total allowable costs to total target cost.

[5] A firm-fixed-price contract provides for a price that is not subject to any adjustment on the basis of the contractor's cost experience in performing the contract. FAR § 16.202-1.

Through DOD's development of a new acquisition strategy in 2011, and in preparation for contract negotiations with ULA, DOD undertook significant efforts to obtain better contractor and subcontractor cost or pricing data. For example, DOD officials and the National Reconnaissance Office cost analysis group collected detailed data on engine prices and subcontractor costs. DOD also scrutinized launch processes to identify and eliminate potentially redundant activities. As a result, DOD contracting officials had a stronger bargaining position to lower overall contract costs than in previous negotiations, and they expect the new contract to realize significant savings primarily through stable unit pricing for all launch vehicles. In June of 2013, they entered into a letter contract with ULA, definitizing the final terms and conditions of the contract in December of 2013. The new contract includes line items for both the fixed-price and cost-reimbursement portions funded under the previous two-contract structure, and DOD officials say the administrative burden of renegotiating every year will be substantially lessened due to the new contract's simplified structure. The new contract is also expected to provide DOD with a better understanding of individual launch costs than it had under previous contracts, as some costs are now directly attributable to specific launches, such as propellants, transportation, and costs associated with launch mission integration. However, according to DOD, about 75 percent of the costs for cost-reimbursement contract items are combined and not broken out by individual launch costs, which may limit DOD's ability to identify the cost of any given launch.

ULA periodically sells launch services to customers outside of the EELV program, such as the National Aeronautics and Space Administration, and to commercial customers. Because DOD pays for ULA's fixed costs, DOD receives compensation for the use of ULA launch services on a per-launch basis for launches ULA sells to non-DOD customers. Prior to the December 2013 contract modification, compensation amounts were loosely based on an average of 30 days of launch pad use, and not based on actual costs. DOD and ULA negotiated the compensation amounts annually, and DOD was reimbursed through price reductions on ULA invoices submitted to DOD at the end of the fiscal year. Under the new contract, compensation is based on some actual costs, including factory support and direct labor hours, and is approximately three times the dollar amount per-launch of reimbursements under previous contracts. Additionally, DOD and ULA plan to adjust the contract value at the outset of each fiscal year, commensurately reducing the overall value by the number of non-DOD launches ULA expects to sell in the upcoming fiscal year.

DOD plans to competitively award contracts for up to 14 launches beginning in fiscal year 2015. Any certified launch provider can compete for the individual missions, including ULA. DOD officials told us they intend to use a best value approach in evaluating proposals from all competitors, meaning factors in addition to price will be considered. For example, DOD may also consider mission risk, taking past performance into account, and satellite vehicle integration risks, including the complexity of integrating the intended satellite or sensor onto each company's launch vehicle. DOD is currently developing its methodology for comparing launch proposals, including establishing how proposals are to be structured, and what the specific evaluation criteria will be. DOD is considering several ways to structure the proposals. If DOD requires all offers to contain both fixed-price and cost-reimbursement features for launch services and capability, respectively, similar to the way it currently contracts with ULA, there could be benefits to DOD and ULA, but potential burdens to new entrants. Alternatively, if DOD implements a fixed-price commercial approach to launch proposals, DOD could lose insight into contractor cost or pricing. DOD could also require a combination of elements from each of these approaches, or develop new contract requirements for this competition. We examined key benefits and challenges of the first two approaches, as they relate to DOD, ULA, and launch companies that would be new entrants. Table 1 summarizes the benefits and challenges to each entity of these two approaches.

Table 1: Potential Procurement Approaches DOD is Considering for Competitive Launch Contract Awards

	Combined Fixed-price Launch Services/Cost-Reimbursement Launch Capability		Fixed-price Commercial	
	Benefits	*Challenges*	*Benefits*	*Challenges*
DOD	DOD is familiar with this approach, has experience negotiating under these terms DOD retains some insight into contractor cost or pricing data which could lend itself to a better bargaining position in future contract negotiations By requiring all companies to submit offers using this structure, DOD would have a straightforward basis on which to compare proposals	DOD use of a cost type contract may negate some efficient contractor business practices and cost savings due to government data requirements under this approach DOD could end up paying for launch capability at more than one launch provider	Cost of contract is identified at the time of award Full and open competition could help to decrease launch prices and increase efficiencies Could facilitate a uniform comparison of launch vehicle prices between companies	DOD access to contractor cost or pricing data would be very limited DOD may lose some flexibility in rescheduling launches if satellite deliveries slip; rearranging launch manifest could add cost Demand for EELV-class launches may diminish after 2018; launch market may not sustain more than one provider
United Launch Alliance (ULA)	DOD funds ULA launch capability to 8 launches; ULA could offer only the additional cost to launch any vehicle above the 8 launches DOD has paid for, giving ULA a price advantage over new entrants ULA would I kely get the benefit of a long history of launch successes ULA is familiar with DOD satellite integration requirements, given its role as the EELV program's sole launch provider	None identified	ULA could phase out business systems fulfilling government cost or pricing data requirements, potentially reducing expenses	ULA's price offer could be higher than new entrant offers, as: • ULA previously stood up business systems to fulfill government cost or pricing data requirements, which would not be required of new entrants under this approach • ULA developed, demonstrated and continues to launch heavy launch vehicles, the most expensive vehicles to build and launch; new entrants are not required to develop and build heavy launch vehicles for this competition
New Entrants	New entrants are not required to develop and demonstrate heavy vehicles to compete for the 14 launches; this could give them a price advantage over ULA Federal Acquisition Regulation prohibits a lack of past performance from being counted against new entrants	DOD does not fund launch capability for new entrants; this could give ULA a price advantage over new entrants Including a cost-reimbursement portion in new entrant launch proposals would require new entrants to develop and install new business systems to fulfill government data requirements	New entrant price offers could be lower than ULA's, as: No added government cost or pricing data requirements would allow companies to keep current business practices Focusing the competition on price considerations without accounting for launch capability costs could help prevent new entrant price offers from rising	None identified

Source: GAO Summary

For additional information on the results of our work, see enclosure I: Briefing on the Space Launch Vehicle Competition. We are not making recommendations in this report.

Agency Comments

We provided a draft of this report to DOD and NRO for comment. DOD provided technical comments that were incorporated as appropriate in the final report. DOD's comments are reproduced in enclosure II: Comments from the Department of Defense.

We are sending copies of this report to the appropriate congressional committees; the Secretary of Defense; and Director of the NRO. This report will also be available at no charge on our website at http://www.gao.gov.

Contact points for our Offices of Congressional Relations and Public Affairs may be found on the last page of this report. Key contributors to this report were Art Gallegos, Assistant Director; Peter Anderson, Claire Buck, Raj Chitikila, Desiree Cunningham, Laura Hook, John Krump, and Roxanna Sun.

Should you or your staff have questions concerning this report, contact Cristina T. Chaplain at (202) 512-4841 or at chaplainc@gao.gov.

Cristina T. Chaplain
Director, Acquisition and Sourcing Management

Enclosure(s) – 2

cc: cc list

(121152)

Space Launch Vehicle Competition

Briefing to the Senate Homeland Security and Governmental Affairs Committee

Permanent Subcommittee on Investigations

January 28, 2014

Page 1

GAO

Contents

- Introduction
- Objectives
- Background
- Findings
- Scope and Methodology

Introduction

- The Department of Defense's Evolved Expendable Launch Vehicle (EELV) program is the primary provider of launch vehicles and services for U.S. military and intelligence satellites. The launch vehicles used by the EELV program are also used to launch civilian and commercial satellites.

- GAO was asked to examine issues related to DOD's effort to introduce competition into EELV acquisitions. Doing so is a significant challenge given the way contracts are currently structured, the fact that new providers are not yet certified to carry sensitive national security satellites and sensors—or payloads—into space, and other complications. The issues GAO was asked to examine include the way that DOD determines costs for launch services with its current contractor and how DOD will compare future offers from different launch services contractors.

Introduction: Program Description and History

- The EELV program started in 1995 when DOD awarded contracts to four companies for preliminary launch vehicle system designs; at that time, DOD's acquisition strategy was to select the one company with the most cost-effective design.

- Given commercial forecasts that predicted sufficient demand to support two launch vehicle providers, in 1997 the Secretary of Defense approved maintaining competition between the two top companies: Lockheed Martin, and what would become Boeing.

- In 2006, following years of projected commercial demand for launch vehicles that did not materialize and increasing launch costs, the two EELV contractors formed a separate company as a joint venture—the United Launch Alliance (ULA).

- From 2006-2013, DOD had two types of contracts with ULA, the sole-source provider, to support the EELV program:
  - a cost-plus-incentive-fee EELV launch capability contract (ELC);[1] and
  - a firm-fixed-price EELV launch services contract (ELS).[2]

1 In July 2011, the EELV program awarded a Launch Capability contract as a cost-plus incentive fee contract; the prior Launch Capability contract was a cost-plus award fee contract. A cost-plus incentive fee contract is a type of cost reimbursement contract that pays the contractor for allowable costs to the extent prescribed in the contract, and allows for the initially negotiated fee to be adjusted later, based on a formula in the contract. The fee is based on the relationship of total allowable costs to total target cost.

2 A firm-fixed-price contract provides for a price that is not subject to any adjustment on the basis of the contractor's cost experience in performing the contract.

Page 4

Introduction: Program Description and History, cont.

- Since 2006, ULA has launched 50 government missions on EELVs, with an extremely high rate of success, and DOD values this reliability. However, in 2010, program cost estimates indicated launch prices were expected to increase at an unsustainable rate, and DOD began an effort to develop a new EELV acquisition strategy.

- The November 2011 strategy was designed to maintain mission success and incentivize price reductions through steady production rates, long-term commitments, opportunities for competition and reductions in workforce redundancy.

- In December 2013, DOD and ULA signed a contract modification, committing DOD to buy 35 launch vehicle booster cores from ULA over a five-year period, and to pay ULA for the associated capability to launch them.[3]

- According to DOD, two primary goals of this long-term sole-source commitment were to increase production stability for ULA and its suppliers, and to reduce the price per launch vehicle.

- The most recent independent cost estimate projects the program will cost close to $70 billion through 2030.[4]

3 The booster core is the main body of a launch vehicle. In the EELV program, common booster cores are used to build all of the Atlas V and Delta IV launch vehicles. Medium and intermediate launch vehicles use one core each, while the Delta IV Heavy launch vehicle requires three.

4 The Office of the Secretary of Defense, Cost Assessment and Program Evaluation conducted an independent cost estimate based on the EELV programmatic forecast dated June 2012.

Page 5

Introduction: Program Description and History, cont.

Figure 1: EELV Program Timeline

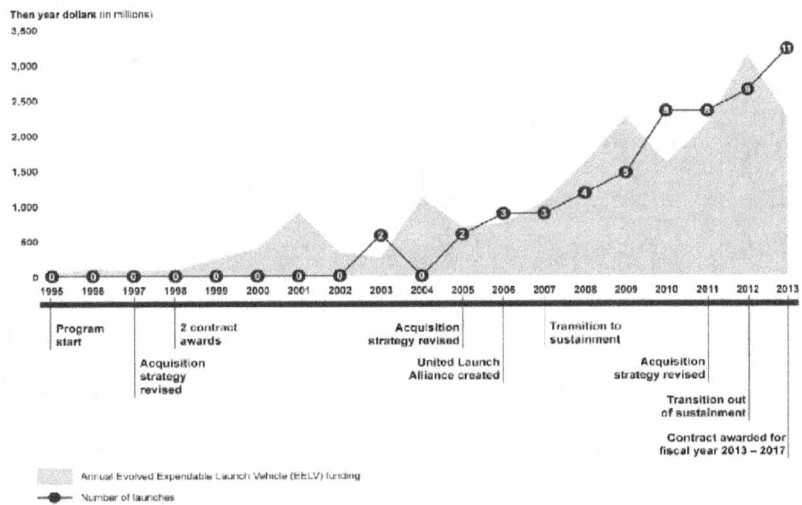

GAO-14-377R Space Launch Competition

Introduction: Reimbursement to DOD for Use of ULA Facilities by Other Customers

- DOD has historically paid all fixed costs for ULA. Prior to the December 2013 contract modification, when ULA sold a launch to another customer, and not through the EELV program office, ULA provided a small reimbursement to DOD for the other customer's use of ULA facilities and infrastructure. There have been concerns that the reimbursement was too small.

Introduction: New Entrants to the Launch Market

- In recent years, companies other than ULA have begun developing new launch vehicles to compete with ULA for EELV-class payloads, and DOD set aside up to 14 launch vehicle booster cores from fiscal years 2015 to 2017 for competition.[5] This competition is expected to begin in fiscal year 2015.

- In order to compete for any of the 14 additional launches these cores represent, new entrant companies have to follow the process outlined by DOD in its Launch Services New Entrant Certification Guide to certify a new vehicle to launch national security missions.

- At this point, none of the likely competitors are able to launch the full range of EELV-class payloads, though at least one company plans to meet the full requirements through further launch vehicle development.

5 EELV-class payloads range from 6,000 to 28,000 lbs to Geosynchronous Transfer Orbit (GTO). They are divided into intermediate (6,000-18,000 lbs to GTO), and heavy (18,000-28,000 lbs to GTO) classes.

Page 8

Introduction: New Entrants, cont.

- Given the use of different contract types and launch vehicle cost allocation practices among contractors, DOD is currently developing a methodology for comparing proposals from all competitors. DOD officials may include this methodology as part of their first request for proposal from launch companies in the competition.

Page 9

GAO

Objectives

This briefing addresses the following questions:

(1) What insight did DOD have into launch costs under past EELV contracts?

(2) How do recent changes to EELV contracts affect accounting for costs?

(3) How is DOD compensated for costs when ULA sells launches to other customers?

(4) What are the implications if DOD requires competitors to submit offers using the same structure it currently uses with ULA or a commercial approach?

Page 10

 **GAO**

Summary of Findings

GAO found:

(1) The previous two-contract structure paid ULA for continuing launch capability to enable the U.S. to readily gain access to space, but one consequence of the structure was that DOD had difficulty determining the cost of an individual launch, as direct launch costs were not separated from other costs.

(2) In the December 2013 EELV contract modification with ULA, DOD leveraged better insight into contractor costs to negotiate lower prices, and incentivized ULA to increase efficiencies, but DOD may have difficulty identifying the total cost of an individual launch.

(3) The December 2013 contract modification stipulates that when ULA sells a launch to customers outside the EELV program office, ULA will adjust the value of the EELV contract by a pre-negotiated amount for each outside launch it sells. Historically the reimbursements have been small compared to the overall launch capability paid for, but DOD recently negotiated larger reimbursements with some direct costs tied to individual launches.

(4) Even with greater insight into contractor costs, DOD may not be immediately poised to take full advantage of competition in the launch market, because, in part, it cannot determine an accurate price for an individual ULA launch.

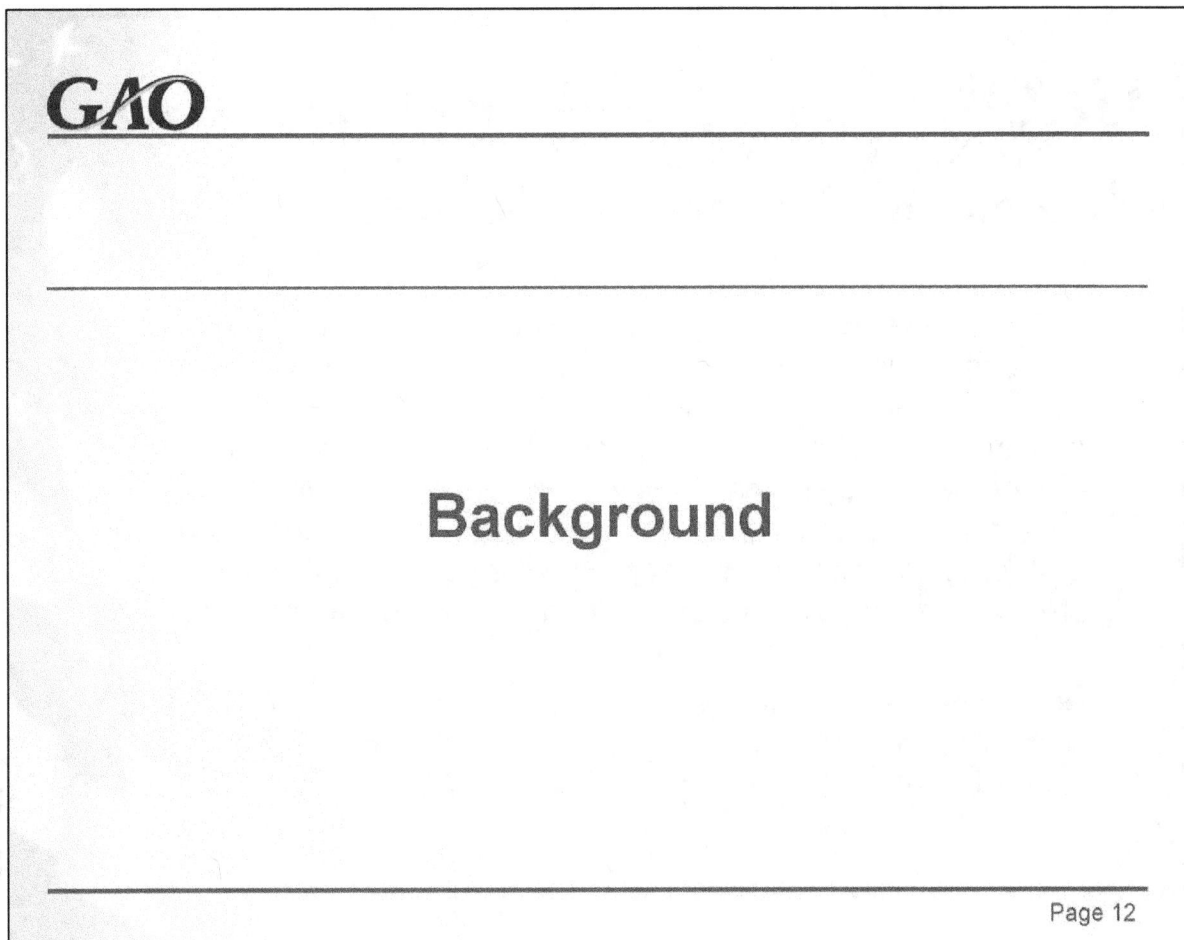

Background

Page 12

Background: Past GAO Findings on EELV

- In 2008, we reported that the EELV program faced numerous oversight challenges, including uncertain launch vehicle reliability, disruption from the consolidation of Boeing and Lockheed Martin manufacturing and operations under the ULA joint venture, and limited programmatic insight due to the elimination of various reporting requirements resulting from the designation of the program as in sustainment. We also reported that DOD was adjusting the EELV budget using premature savings estimates, and made three recommendations to improve DOD oversight.

- DOD reinstated reporting requirements and completed a new life-cycle cost estimate, but did not assess the EELV program's staffing needs to confirm whether shortages exist (GAO-08-1039).

Page 13

Background: Past GAO Findings on EELV, cont.

- In 2011, we found that DOD was using insufficient data, particularly data on costs and on the launch industrial base, and relying on contractor-supplied information to inform the development of a new EELV acquisition strategy. We recommended seven actions that would help address critical knowledge gaps.

- In response, DOD reassessed the block buy contract, examined broader launch issues, incentivized the contractor to implement efficiencies without affecting mission success, indicated it does not intend to waive future data requirements, is working with the National Aeronautics and Space Administration (NASA) on heavy launch decisions and conducting an independent assessment of the launch industrial base, but has not developed a science and technology plan for evolving launch technologies (GAO-11-641).

Page 14

Background: Past GAO Findings on EELV, cont.

- In 2012, we reported that DOD had numerous efforts in progress to address the knowledge gaps and data deficiencies we identified in our 2011 report, and that these improvements would allow DOD to make more informed decisions on how to proceed with the EELV program (GAO-12-822).

- Additionally, in 2013, we reported that DOD's implementation of its New Entrant Certification Guide, while generally satisfactory to the new entrants, posed some challenges to launch vehicle certification (GAO-13-317R).

Page 15

Objective 1:
Accounting for Costs Under Past EELV Contracts

GAO

Objective 1: Accounting for Costs under Past EELV Contracts
Reasons for the Two-contract Structure

In 2005, DOD modified the way it contracted for EELV launches.

- The need for flexibility in launch schedules encouraged DOD to pay for launch capability (primarily labor) separately from the launch hardware, as DOD wanted to avoid additional costs associated with the frequent launch delays they were experiencing as new satellites were being developed and produced.[6]

By paying for a capability to launch, or "standing army" of personnel (particularly engineers), separately from the launch hardware, DOD believed it was ensuring itself access to space in a timely manner, regardless of payload delays.

6 We have frequently reported that many of these satellite development and production delays could have been reduced or avoided by using best practices in space acquisition processes.

Page 17

Objective 1: Accounting for Costs under Past EELV Contracts
Basic Contract Structure of Past EELV Contracts

From 2006-2013, ULA had two types of contracts with DOD through which it provided launch services for national security space launches:

- EELV launch capability (ELC): cost-reimbursement contracts which funded items that, according to DOD officials, were not easily acquired under a fixed-price contract, such as overhead on launch pads and engineering support.[7]

- EELV launch services (ELS): firm-fixed-price contracts that paid for launch vehicle hardware and labor directly associated with building and assembling launch vehicles.

---

7 As previously noted, in July 2011 DOD awarded a Launch Capability contract as a cost-plus incentive fee contract; prior to that award, the contract was a cost-plus award fee contract.

Page 18

Objective 1: Accounting for Costs under Past EELV Contracts

Table 1: Details of the EELV Two-contract Structure

	EELV Launch Capability (ELC)	EELV Launch Services (ELS)
Contract type	Cost-plus incentive fee	Firm-fixed-price
Purpose	To acquire launch capability - the "standing army" required to maintain assured access to space for 8 launches per year.	To acquire launch hardware.
Items covered by the contract	Includes items not included in ELS such as: mission integration, systems engineering, production management, propellants, transportation, labor to conduct launches, etc.	Launch vehicle hardware, production, and directly associated touch labor.
Number of active contracts	Only one contract active at any time.	Multiple contracts with ULA active at any time.
Length of contract term	The contract covers one year of launch capability.	Varies; ELS contracts can be for one launch or multiple launches, and some can last for many years as the launches included in the contract are launched.

Source: GAO analysis of DOD contracts and related documents, and discussions with DOD officials

Page 19

Objective 1: Accounting for Costs under Past EELV Contracts Obscured Costs under the Two-contract Structure

ELC contracts did not require the contractor to break out costs associated with each launch, therefore, DOD was unable to calculate specific costs for individual EELV launch missions. For example, while each of the following costs could have been tied directly to an individual launch, DOD contracting officials included these items in the scope of the ELC—a cost-type contract—but did not require the contractor to separate them by individual launch:

- Propellants – fuel expenses for each launch.

- Transportation – the cost of transporting a completed launch vehicle from the factory to the launch site.

- Mission integration – the work involved in mating the satellite to the launch vehicle could be tied to the overall costs of a specific launch.

Objective 1: Accounting for Costs under Past EELV Contracts Challenges Encountered under the ELC/ELS Structure

The EELV program under the ELC/ELS structure had some significant outcomes, but presented challenges to the program:

- Through the ULA joint venture and subsequent consolidation of operations, the government realized some significant savings. However, given the lack of incentive to identify efficiencies in the program's prior cost-reimbursement contract structure, and in an environment where no viable competition existed, program cost estimates showed launch prices were expected to rise.

- The program earned a record of consistent launch successes but, according to DOD, the focus of the program became primarily mission success, and not efficiencies or cost savings.

- According to DOD officials, the ELC contract structure was not transparent, and DOD had limited insight into some contractor costs, leading to:
  - insufficient knowledge to negotiate fair and reasonable launch prices,
  - lack of understanding of the total costs of any given launch, and
  - inadequate ability to account for costs reimbursed to DOD when ULA sold launches to non-DOD customers.

Page 21

Objective 2:
Recent Changes to EELV Contracts and Impacts

Objective 2: Recent Changes to EELV Contracts and Impacts
Better Information to Support Contract Negotiations

- As part of its effort to re-evaluate the EELV acquisition strategy, DOD has taken significant steps between 2010 and 2013 to obtain information to help it better identify the costs of EELV launches, and has made progress in reducing contract prices.

- We reported in 2012 that detailed investigations, or "deep-dives," into engine prices and other subcontractor costs have provided DOD better information with which to support contract negotiations with ULA. This insight was absent in past contract negotiations, in part because DOD waived rights to some contractor data in exchange for lower prices from large commercial hardware purchases.

- Additionally, DOD has scrutinized launch processes to identify and eliminate potentially redundant activities.

Page 23

GAO-14-377R Space Launch Competition

Objective 2: Recent Changes to EELV Contracts and Impacts
Better Information to Support Contract Negotiations, cont.

- DOD had better information in its recent contract negotiations with ULA, affording DOD a stronger bargaining position to lower overall contract costs than in recent years. As noted earlier, we recommended DOD obtain better data to strengthen DOD's bargaining position.

- Gaining greater insight into contractor costs and reducing inefficiencies could have also benefited the program from the start of the joint venture in 2006, as program costs continued to rise.

- Additionally, we reported in 2011 that competition could spur ULA efficiencies and incentivize ULA pricing. The presence of potential competition for launch services—a recent development—likely provided the context to help DOD negotiate lower prices.

Page 24

Objective 2: Recent Changes to EELV Contracts and Impacts
Key Tenets of the New Contract

The December 2013 contract modification with ULA, sometimes referred to as a "block buy" contract, represents a major change from past year-to-year contracting approaches, and buys:

- Production of 35 launch vehicle booster cores over 5 years, from fiscal years 2013 through 2017
- Launch capability for six years, from fiscal years 2014 through 2019

Instead of two separate ELC/ELS contracts, the new single contract structure covers the entire EELV program, with contract line items for different aspects of the program, such as:

- launch vehicle hardware
- launch capability, including systems engineering and production management
- mission integration
- propellants

Page 25

Objective 2: Recent Changes to EELV Contracts and Impacts Key Tenets, cont.

According to DOD, some changes to the modified contract include:

- Better attribution of direct costs to launch vehicles, such as propellants and mission integration, into separate contract line items.
- More representative compensation to DOD when ULA sells a launch to a non-DOD customer
  - Compensation to DOD is roughly three times what it was under previous contracts with ULA (dollar amount is proprietary).
- DOD officials estimate about $4.4 billion savings over the fiscal year 2012 President's Budget estimate.
- Stable unit pricing for all launch vehicles.

However, while DOD can identify the cost of launch capability by year, it may be unable to determine the total cost of an individual launch because the majority of launch capability costs are not allocated to individual launches. Additionally, according to DOD, it is to pay for launch capability for 8 launches, even if fewer launches actually take place that year.

Page 26

Objective 3: Compensation to DOD for Non-DOD Launches

Objective 3: Compensation to DOD for Non-DOD Launches
Historical Reimbursements

- The 2004 U.S. Space Transportation Policy instructed DOD to fully fund the fixed costs of the EELV program. However, the 2013 National Space Transportation Policy does not instruct DOD to fully fund the fixed costs of the EELV program.
- Prior to the December 2013 contract modification,
  - ULA provided a small reimbursement to DOD for the resources used to launch missions sold to other customers, such as NASA or other government or commercial customers.
  - DOD and ULA annually negotiated the value of the reimbursement.
  - Reimbursements, also known as offsets:
    - represented the average 30-day cost of launch vehicles boosters on the launch pad for a given fiscal year, and not actual expenses.
    - differed based on which launch vehicle is used, and from which launch range the vehicle is flown.
    - were made through price reductions on the invoices ULA submitted to DOD.

Page 28

Objective 3: Compensation to DOD for Non-DOD Launches Changes Under the December 2013 EELV Contract Modification

- According to DOD officials, the December 2013 contract modification changes how launches sold to other customers are handled.
- One significant change is the method by which DOD is to be compensated when ULA sells launches to other customers. Specifically, ULA and DOD will adjust the EELV contract value at the start of each fiscal year, based on the number of non-DOD launches ULA expects to sell that year.
- DOD officials told us the EELV program intends to pay only for the capability it requires, that is, 8 launches per year for the duration of the contract.
- The contract also includes provisions for more representative compensation for non-DOD launches. For example, compensation to DOD will:
  - be based in part on discrete, allocable costs per launch, and
  - amount to roughly three times what is was under previous contracts, though it still represents a small percentage of total capability paid for
- Although DOD negotiated larger dollar amounts in the current contract, DOD may not know if it is receiving fair and representative compensation because many ELC costs are not allocated by launch.

Objective 4:
Implications of Requiring Competitors to Bid Launch Proposals Using an ELC/ELS Structure or Commercial Approach

Page 30

Objective 4: Implications of Requiring Competitors to Bid Launch Proposals Using an ELC/ELS Structure or Commercial Approach
Best Value Comparison

Based on our discussions with DOD, DOD plans to conduct a best value procurement where price is not the only consideration. DOD will likely consider several factors when comparing proposals for up to14 additional launches available for competition between ULA and new entrants, including the following:

- Price—companies may be required to offer proposals that include capability (cost-reimbursement) and launch hardware (fixed-price) components, similar to the current ELC/ELS contract structure with ULA;

- Mission risk—DOD will likely take past launch performance into account;

- Mission integration—DOD will likely consider any additional work required to integrate satellites onto each company's launch vehicles.

DOD has not yet decided whether to require competitors to submit offers using an ELC/ELS structure, a commercial approach, or some other type of proposal.

Objective 4: Implications to DOD of Requiring an ELC/ELS Structure for Launch Proposals

Benefits to DOD

•DOD is familiar and experienced with the ELC/ELS approach of funding launches; this approach would not disrupt the current contractual arrangement with ULA.

•By requiring all companies to bid using an ELC/ELS structure, DOD would have a straightforward basis on which to compare proposals.

•Greater insight into contractor cost or pricing data could lend itself to a better bargaining position in future contract negotiations.

Challenges to DOD

•DOD has greater insight into current EELV costs than in the past, but may find itself funding an under-utilized launch capability with ULA if they select a new entrant for some or all of the 14 launches. This is because the current contract pays for annual ULA launch capability for 8 launches, even if fewer launches actually take place in a given year. If DOD buys a launch from another provider, it may be paying for duplicate capabilities.

•Allowing new entrants to compete on a commercial, fixed-price basis could yield more efficient business practices and cost savings to DOD than it would otherwise obtain through cost-type contracts. This is because government cost-type contracts require more data and government insight than commercial contracts, which can be expensive.

Objective 4: Implications to ULA if DOD Requires an ELC/ELS Structure for Launch Proposals

Benefits to ULA	Challenges to ULA
•DOD's recent block buy contract with ULA buys launch capability for six years, and affords ULA the opportunity to offer only the incremental cost to ULA of launching any of the 14 available missions. This is because under the current EELV contract, DOD has already bought ULA launch capability for 8 launches per year, even if fewer launches actually take place.	•New entrants are expected to compete for up to 14 launches before they have been certified to launch the full range of EELV missions, meaning they have not paid the developmental costs of standing up their heavy launch vehicles and pads. This could give new entrants a price advantage over ULA, which is required to provide launch services for all variants of EELVs, including heavy launch vehicles, the most expensive to build and launch.
•ULA may get the benefit of an excellent launch record of 67 consecutive successful launches of government (defense and civil) and commercial missions on Atlas V and Delta IV launch vehicles since 2002.[8]	
•Satellite integration requirements for ULA's Atlas V and Delta IV launch vehicles are generally known, given ULA's role as the EELV program's sole launch provider.	

8 Lockheed Martin and Boeing launched Atlas V and Delta IV launch vehicles, respectively, beginning in 2002, prior to the formation of ULA in 2006.

Page 33

Objective 4: Implications to New Entrants if DOD Requires an ELC/ELS Structure for Launch Proposals

Benefits to new entrants

•New entrants are expected to compete for up to 14 launches before becoming certified to conduct the full range of EELV missions. This affords them a potential price advantage over ULA, as new providers have not yet had to pay for the development, production, and demonstration of each type of launch vehicle.

•While new entrants cannot demonstrate a long past performance record for EELV-class launches as can ULA, the Federal Acquisition Regulation (FAR) prohibits a lack of a performance history from being considered a negative.[9]

Challenges to new entrants

•DOD does not currently fund launch capability for new entrant companies, as it does for ULA. If DOD requires a similar structure for new entrants, they may ultimately have to stand up their own capability to meet DOD requirements, which could be costly.

•New entrants prefer to submit proposals on a commercial, fixed-price basis instead of duplicating ULA's ELC/ELS business model, which they view as inefficient and expensive. Particularly, the cost-reimbursement portion of the contract would require development and installation of business systems to gather required data, at additional cost to the new entrants.

9 FAR §15.305(a)(2)(iv).

Page 34

Objective 4: Using a Commercial Approach for Launch Proposals

- New entrants would prefer to submit proposals on a commercial, fixed-price basis in accordance with FAR Part 12, in order to focus the EELV competition on price without DOD having to pay separately for ELC costs.[10]

- DOD is reluctant to use a FAR Part 12 approach because DOD believes this approach limits DOD's insight into contractor costs. Officials indicate a lack of insight into these costs led to problems in the past.

- DOD also points out that a FAR Part 12 approach would have fewer cost and data reporting requirements for new entrants than are currently placed on ULA, leading to an unfair cost advantage for the new entrants who would not have to develop and install business systems to manage a cost-reimbursement contract.

- However, if a robust competitive environment exists in the post-block buy phase beginning in fiscal year 2018, DOD has noted that it may depart from the ELC/ELS construct while requiring all companies to submit offers in a full and open competition for launch services.

10 FAR Part 12 outlines processes for acquiring commercial items, which are defined as items that are customarily used by the general public or by non-governmental entities for purposes other than governmental purposes. Some features of FAR Part 12 contracts include less insight into cost or pricing data, and fixed-price contract types.

Page 35

Objective 4: Using a Commercial Approach, cont.

Potential benefits to DOD	Potential challenges to DOD
•Use of a fixed-price contract identifies the cost of the contract at time of award.	•Under a fixed-price commercial-type contract, DOD access to cost data would be very limited.
•Could facilitate a straightforward comparison of launch vehicle prices between companies without having to account for ULA's ELC contract structure.	•DOD believes there may not be sufficient demand in fiscal year 2018 and beyond to support multiple launch providers.
•Full and open competition could help to decrease launch prices and increase efficiencies.	•Given the national imperative for an assured access to space, DOD may be forced to continue funding for launch capability if multiple launch providers cannot be sustained by the launch market, making a commercial approach impractical.
	•DOD may lose some flexibility in its launch schedule, as rearranging and rescheduling launches due to satellite delays or other factors could incur added cost, according to DOD officials.

Scope and Methodology

We interviewed or obtained information from:

- Air Force Space Command, Peterson Air Force Base, Colorado Springs, Colorado
- Air Force Space and Missile Systems Center, Launch Systems Directorate, Los Angeles Air Force Base, El Segundo, California
- Defense Contract Audit Agency, Littleton, Colorado
- Defense Contract Management Agency, Littleton, Colorado
- Office of the Secretary of Defense, Cost Assessment and Program Evaluation, Washington, District of Columbia
- Orbital Sciences Corporation, El Segundo, California
- Program Executive Officer for Space Launch, Washington, District of Columbia
- Space Exploration Technologies, Inc., Hawthorne, California
- United Launch Alliance, Centennial, Colorado

Page 37

Scope and Methodology, cont.

To determine the insight DOD had into launch costs under past EELV contracts:
- We reviewed the two most recent ELC and ELS contracts and examined the contract structure and breakdown of costs included in the contract.
- We received an in-depth verbal and written briefing on the ELC contract from DOD, and discussed with senior Air Force officials the history, context, and makeup of the EELV contracts.
- We interviewed other DOD and incumbent contractor officials regarding direct launch vehicle and other supporting activities performed under the contracts.
- We reviewed Defense Contract Audit Agency audit reports of EELV launch contracts, report dates ranging from 2005 to 2012.
- We reviewed past GAO reports and identified previous recommendations and their implementation to determine DOD insight into contracts.

To determine how recent changes to EELV contracts affect accounting for costs:
- We discussed the new EELV contract with DOD contracting officials and received an in-depth briefing on the structure of the new contract, including changes from previous contracts.
- We reviewed the modified EELV contract, and compared its contents and dollar amounts to previous versions of EELV contracts.
- We discussed the modified EELV contract, and changes from previous contracts, with the incumbent contractor.

Page 38

Scope and Methodology, cont.

To determine how DOD is reimbursed for costs when the incumbent provider sells launches to other customers:
- We examined ELC contracts from fiscal years 2012-2014 to determine reimbursements.
- We interviewed DOD and incumbent contractor officials to identify how any reimbursement amounts were calculated and the extent to which ELC costs were included.
- We analyzed the reimbursement amounts and calculated the percentages of total ELC costs that the reimbursements represented annually.

To determine the implications of possible DOD approaches to comparing launch proposals between the incumbent and new launch providers:
- We discussed DOD's plans to make the comparison in interviews with DOD officials who are developing the plan.
- We reviewed draft DOD performance work statement related to the proposed EELV competition.
- We discussed the implications of DOD's plan with DOD officials, new entrant launch service providers and the incumbent provider.
- We reviewed FAR requirements for various types of contracts, including fixed-price and cost—reimbursement-type contracts.

We obtained technical comments from DOD to ensure the accuracy of the slides, and incorporated changes as appropriate.

Page 39

GAO on the Web
Web site: http://www.gao.gov/

Congressional Relations
Katherine Siggerud, Managing Director, siggerudk@gao.gov
(202) 512-4400, U.S. Government Accountability Office
441 G Street, NW, Room 7125, Washington, DC 20548

Public Affairs
Chuck Young, Managing Director, youngc1@gao.gov
(202) 512-4800, U.S. Government Accountability Office
441 G Street, NW, Room 7149, Washington, DC 20548

Copyright

Page 40

DEPARTMENT OF THE AIR FORCE
WASHINGTON, DC

Office Of The Assistant Secretary

SAF/AQS
1060 Air Force Pentagon
Washington, DC 20330-1060

Ms. Cristina Chaplain
Director, Acquisition and Sourcing Management
U.S. Government Accountability Office
441 G. Street, N.W.
Washington D.C. 20548

Dear Ms. Chaplain:

This is the Department of Defense (DoD) response to the GAO Draft Report, GAO-14-377R, 'The Air Force's Evolved Expendable Launch Vehicle Competitive Procurement,' dated February 24, 2014 (GAO Code 121152). The Department appreciates the opportunity to review the GAO briefing and findings as we continue our efforts to introduce competition into the Evolved Expendable Launch Vehicle (EELV) program.

The Air Force intends to establish a competition that complies with the Federal Acquisition Regulation, treats all competitors fairly, and aggressively pursues a good deal for the United States Government.

Should you have questions or need additional information please contact Major Kyle Allen, (703) 695-3511, kyle.s.allen2.mil@mail.mil.

Sincerely,

ROBERT D. MCMURRY, Maj Gen, USAF
Director, Space Programs
Assistant Secretary (Acquisition)

www.ingramcontent.com/pod-product-compliance
Lightning Source LLC
Chambersburg PA
CBHW080623290526
45790CB00007B/2906